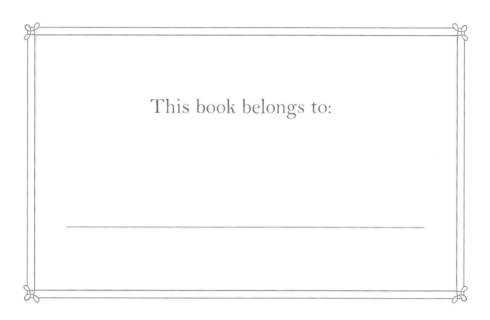

This book belongs to:

_____

THE WONDERFUL WORLD OF

ZURI
ROSE

*To Zuri, who is my love,
my life, and my light*

*For my grandmothers, Paulina and
Beryl, who introduced me to the
wonderful world of flowers*

Text copyright © 2022 by Makini Regal Martin
Illustrations copyright © 2022 by Haley Moss

Typeset in Bell and Didot

ISBN: 9781638190899

First Edition

Printed in China

10 9 8 7 6 5 4 3 2 1

BLOOMHAUS
PRESS
— EST 2021 —

Published by BloomHaus Press

www.bloomhauspress.com

Follow @makiniregal and @worldofzurirose on Instagram.

THE WONDERFUL WORLD OF

ZURI ROSE

MAKINI REGAL MARTIN

ILLUSTRATED BY HALEY MOSS

My name is Zuri Rose, but my friends call me Zu Zu. I love flowers—like really, really love them. I learned all about flowers from my mum. She owns a flower shop in New York City's flower district.

On Saturday mornings, we leave our Brooklyn brownstone to head to the flower district in Manhattan. The flower district is filled with lots of flower shops and the most beautiful flowers from all around the world.

I have so many favorite flowers. It's hard to pick just one. I would love to share some of my favorites with you!

A IS FOR ALLIUM

a·lee·uhm

Alliums look like giant pom-poms. When I say giant, I mean *huge!* They can be as big as basketballs and can grow up to four feet tall. That's even taller than I am!

B IS FOR BIRD-OF-PARADISE

burd uhv peh·ruh·dais

Want to know what my favorite bird is? The bird-of-paradise! I know it's not a real bird, but doesn't it look like one? My Great Granny Paulina grows them in her garden on the twin islands of Trinidad and Tobago.

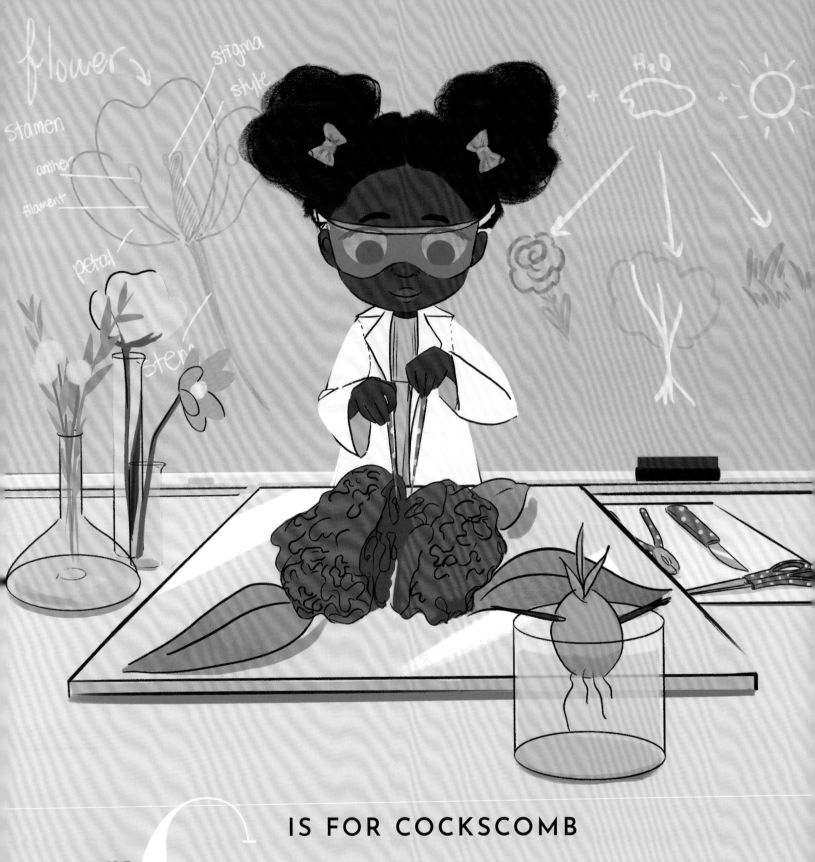

IS FOR COCKSCOMB

kaak·skowm

My favorite thing about science class is learning about the brain. And my favorite thing about the cockscomb flower is that it *looks* like a brain! That's why it's also called brain *Celosia*. It has a swirly, brain-like texture.

D IS FOR DAHLIA

da·lee·uh

Guess what? All of these flowers are dahlias! Some are itty bitty and look like buttons. The other ones are as big as dinner plates! My favorite dahlias are café au lait, a creamy pink color that often gets used at weddings. So pretty!

IS FOR ENGLISH BLUEBELL

ing·gluhsh bloo·bel

English bluebells are native to England. All of their flowers are on the same side of the stalk. They get their names because they look like little bells. I wonder if they make music only bees can hear!

F IS FOR FREESIA

free·zhuh

Mmm . . . do you smell that? It's freesia, and it's coming from my soap! Freesia's petals are also used to create perfume, lotion, and makeup. Mum and I love having at-home spa days with our favorite freesia products.

G IS FOR GARDENIA

gaar·dee·nyuh

These delicate blooms have a waxy texture and glossy, emerald leaves. I like to wear gardenias in my hair, just like my daddy's favorite jazz singer Billie Holiday. He said with more singing lessons, I can sing like her!

H

IS FOR HIBISCUS

hai·bis·kuhs

I love the hibiscus, but not as much as hummingbirds do. Those fast-moving birds fly around pollinating the colorful, trumpet-shaped flowers. You know what else is cool? The hibiscus is the national flower of Haiti. Its petals are also used to make a yummy drink called sorrel.

I IS FOR IRIS

ai·ruhs

Irises, named after the Greek goddess of the rainbow, bloom in vibrant shades like purple, blue, and yellow. Irises can be bearded or beardless because of the fuzzy hairlike texture on their petals. I wonder how I would look with a beard!

J IS FOR JASMINE

jaz·muhn

Do you know what my favorite drink is? It's chocolate oat milk, but jasmine tea is a close second! This delicious, fragrant tea is made from jasmine petals. When I have tea parties, my mum makes jasmine tea for my friends and me.

K IS FOR KING PROTEA

king prow·tee·uh

Have you ever eaten an artichoke? Well, king protea looks like an artichoke, but you can't eat it because it's poisonous. It's also South Africa's national flower and has the largest head of its kind.

L IS FOR LAVENDER

la·vuhn·dr

Did you know that lavender can make you feel better when you're sick? Really! It can calm you down and help you sleep better. The most beautiful lavender fields in the world are in Provence, France.

M

IS FOR MIMOSA

muh·mow·suh

Kangaroos and koala bears aren't the only things that come from Australia. Mimosas do, too! They grow on trees and only flower in the winter. They're the cutest little yellow blooms that look like mini pom-poms.

IS FOR NYMPHAEA

nim·fei·uh

Nymphaeas, or water lilies, are large floating plants with white or pink flowers and round lily pads. Frogs love them because they're the perfect hiding spot from water snakes in search of their next meal. Frogs for lunch? No way!

IS FOR ORCHID

or·kuhd

There are more types of orchids than there are animals on our planet. Imagine that! I love *Phalaenopsis,* or "phals" for short, because they're my Grandma Doretha's favorite houseplants. She always has a ton of them in her sunroom.

IS FOR PEONY

pee·uh·nee

When I was a flower girl in my Aunty Nia's wedding, I had a beautiful, blush pink peony bouquet. It looked and smelled like cotton candy. Peonies are popular at weddings because they symbolize luck and love. Swoon!

IS FOR QUEEN ANNE'S LACE

Kween anz leis

What's your favorite vegetable? I like carrots, which is why I love Queen Anne's lace, also called wild carrot. This frilly wildflower looks like a beautiful piece of lace. That's why it's named after Queen Anne of Denmark, who was an expert lacemaker.

IS FOR QUEEN ANNE'S LACE

IS FOR ROSE

rohz

Can you guess why my name is Zuri Rose? No, it's not because I smell as sweet as a rose. It's because my nana's name is Rose. Did you know that roses are the national flower of the United States? There are tiny roses called spray roses and larger ones with ruffles called garden roses.

IS FOR SUNFLOWER

suhn·flaw·ur

Did you know that sunflowers can grow as tall as sixteen feet? That's almost four of me! Sunflowers also taste delish. That's right! You can eat their seeds, which are so yummy and good for you!

SUNFLR

IS FOR TULIPS

too·luhps

Holland is the capital of tulips. There are more than one hundred species of tulips. Close your eyes and imagine being in a field of thousands of tulips in every color of the rainbow. Magical, isn't it? Tulips only bloom in the springtime, so enjoy them while they last!

U IS FOR URSINIA

ur·sin·ia

Do you know who loves *Ursinias* more than I do?
Bees! Bees love them because of their brilliant
yellowy-orange color and sweet nectar. *Ursinias* grow
in South Africa and are also called African daisies.

V IS FOR VIOLET

vai·luht

Violets—also known as Violas—have heart-shaped leaves. There's a famous poem about violets. Have you ever heard it? "Roses are red, violets are blue, flowers smell sweet, and sometimes make me go achoo!"

IS FOR WISTERIA

wuh·stee·ree·uh

Do you love climbing trees? If so, then you're in great company because Wisterias love climbing, too! They like tall buildings the most! Wisterias can also live more than one hundred years! That's even older than my papa, and he's *really* old.

X IS FOR XERANTHEMUM

xe·ran·the·mum

Xeranthemum, Xeranthemum, Xeranthemum! Wow! That's a bit of a tongue twister. Xeranthemums are known as everlasting flowers. Even after they've dried, they keep their shape and color, so they last forever and ever. Pretty cool, huh?

Y IS FOR YELLOW-EYED GRASS

yeh·low aid gras

What color are your eyes? Mine are brown. I don't know anyone with yellow eyes. Do you? Yellow-eyed grass actually isn't a flower. It's a plant with grassy leaves and yellow flowers at its tip.

Z IS FOR ZINNIA

zin·nia

If you love butterflies as much as I do, then you'll love *Zinnias!* They're often planted in butterfly gardens. Can you imagine being surrounded by beautiful butterflies and flowers?

Well, that's it. These are all my favorite flowers from A–Z! I hope you enjoyed learning about the wonderful world of flowers! What was your favorite flower?

I can't wait to share more fun things with you—like when I was a flower girl for the first time and when I went to Trinidad for the world-famous carnival.

Please send me pictures of you and your favorite flowers, with your grown-up's permission of course! You can email me at hello@thewonderfulworldofzurirose.com or tag me on Instagram @worldofzurirose. Can't wait to hear from you!

'Till next time, friends!

xoxo,

Zuri Rose

BOTANICAL FLOWER NAMES

Each flower has a common name and a botanical name, which is the scientific Latin name that identifies the group (genus) and species of the flower. Some flowers have the same name for both, which is pretty cool.

Allium	*Allium*
Bird-of-Paradise	*Strelitzia*
Cockscomb	*Celosia*
Dahlia	*Dahlia*
English Bluebell	*Hyacinthoides non-scripta*
Freesia	*Freesia*
Gardenia	*Gardenia jasminoides*
Hibiscus	*Hibiscus*
Iris	*Iris*
Jasmine	*Jasminum*
King Protea	*Protea cynaroides*
Lavender	*Lavandula*
Mimosa	*Acacia*
Nymphaea	*Water Lily*
Orchid	*Phalaenopsis*
Peony	*Paeonia*
Queen Anne's Lace	*Daucus carota*
Rose	*Rosa carolina*
Sunflower	*Helianthus*
Tulip	*Tulipa*
Ursinia	*Ursinia*
Violet	*Viola*
Wisteria	*Wisteria sinensis*
Xeranthemum	*Xeranthemum annuum*
Zinnia	*Zinnia*

Makini Regal Martin is a published floral, event, and interior designer. Trinidadian-born and Brooklyn-bred, Makini always possessed a natural gift for design. She inherited her love for flowers from her two grandmothers, both avid gardeners and flower enthusiasts. After graduating from Columbia University and honing a successful career in management consulting, Makini turned her keen eye for design and love of flowers into a blossoming business when she launched Makini Regal Designs in 2011. Her design work has been published by New York Magazine, Essence, Design Sponge, The Knot, Munaluchi Bride, Black Enterprise, and many others. After the birth of her daughter, Zuri Rose, Makini was inspired to launch a lifestyle blog and write a children's book series. The Wonderful World of Zuri Rose: Flowers A–Z is the first book of that series. When not immersed in all things flowers and design, Makini spends her days in her Brooklyn brownstone with her husband, Jason, and daughter. You can find Makini on Instagram @makiniregal.